NATIVE AMERICAN BIOGRAPHIES

THE LIFE OF
CRAZY HORSE

MIRIAM COLEMAN

PowerKiDS
press.

New York

Published in 2017 by The Rosen Publishing Group, Inc.
29 East 21st Street, New York, NY 10010

First Edition

Editor: Sarah Machajewski
Book Design: Katelyn Heinle/Tanya Dellaccio

Photo Credits: Cover (monument) Marka/Universal Images Group/Getty Images; cover (backdrop) Wollertz/Shutterstock.com; p. 5 Jean-Marc Giboux/Hulton Archive/Getty Images; p. 7 courtesy of Library of Congress; p. 9 Simon Scott/Moment/Getty Images; p. 10 Carolina K. Smith MD/Shutterstock.com; p. 11 Jack Dean III/Shutterstock.com; p. 12 https://en.wikipedia.org/wiki/Bozeman_Trail#/media/File:BozemanTrailPhilKonstantin.jpg; p. 13 (main) https://en.wikipedia.org/wiki/Fort_Phil_Kearny#/media/File:Fort_Phil_Kearney.jpg; p. 13 (inset) https://en.wikipedia.org/wiki/Fort_Phil_Kearny#/media/File:FortPhillipKearney.jpg; p. 14 https://en.wikipedia.org/wiki/Sioux#/media/File:Great_Sioux_reservation_in_1888.png; p. 15 MPI/Moment/Getty Images; p. 17 Hulton Archive/Staff/Getty Images; p. 18 https://en.wikipedia.org/wiki/George_Crook#/media/File:George_Crook_-_Brady-Handy.jpg; p. 19 Print Collector/Hulton Fine Art Collection/Getty Images; p. 20 https://en.wikipedia.org/wiki/George_Armstrong_Custer#/media/File:Custer_Bvt_MG_Geo_A_1865_LC-BH831-365-crop.jpg; p. 21 https://en.wikipedia.org/wiki/Battle_of_the_Little_Bighorn#/media/File:Charles_Marion_Russell_-_The_Custer_Fight_(1903).jpg; p. 23 Interim Archives/Archive Photos/Getty Images; p. 25 https://en.wikipedia.org/wiki/Crazy_Horse#/media/File:Ftrob_ch.jpg; p. 27 https://en.wikipedia.org/wiki/Crazy_Horse_Memorial#/media/File:Crazy_Horse_Memorial_2010.jpg; p. 29 AWL Images/Getty Images.

Library of Congress Cataloging-in-Publication Data

Coleman, Miriam, author.
The life of Crazy Horse / Miriam Coleman.
    pages cm. — (Native American biographies)
Includes index.
ISBN 978-1-5081-4825-8 (pbk.)
ISBN 978-1-5081-4780-0 (6 pack)
ISBN 978-1-5081-4815-9 (library binding)
1. Crazy Horse, approximately 1842-1877—Juvenile literature. 2. Oglala Indians—Kings and rulers—Biography—Juvenile literature. 3. Oglala Indians—History—Juvenile literature. I. Title.
E99.O3C722128 2016
973.8'3092—dc23
                                    2015036310

Manufactured in the United States of America

CPSIA Compliance Information: Batch #BS16PK: For Further Information contact Rosen Publishing, New York, New York at 1-800-237-9932

CONTENTS

THE FACE IN THE MOUNTAIN

In the Black Hills of South Dakota, rising above the pine trees, a monument is being created that will be more than 500 feet (152 m) high when it's finished. The monument honors Crazy Horse, who was a leader of the Lakota people.

To much of the world, Crazy Horse is known as the fierce warrior who helped defeat U.S. forces at the Battle of the Little Bighorn. Throughout history, he has been admired for his refusal to compromise and his unwillingness to give up the Lakotas' **traditional** ways of life on the Great Plains. Crazy Horse's powerful fighting skills may have made him famous, but his commitment to his principles made him a hero.

The Crazy Horse Memorial helps keep Crazy Horse's memory alive.

A LAKOTA CHILDHOOD

Crazy Horse was born around 1840 near present-day Rapid City, South Dakota. His father, who was also named Crazy Horse, was from the Oglala band of Lakotas. His mother came from the Miniconjou people, which was another branch of the Lakotas. As a child, Crazy Horse was called "Curly Hair" or "Light Hair" for his uncommonly brown, wavy hair.

Crazy Horse grew up roaming the Great Plains with the Oglalas, following the bison herds between the Black Hills of South Dakota and the North Platte River in Wyoming. He joined in bison hunts from the time he was a small boy and became skilled at riding and shooting by the age of 10. He had a particular talent for capturing and taming wild horses, as well as stealing horses from other tribes.

This photo, dated to 1891, shows some traditional aspects of Lakota life, including clothing and a tepee. One woman carries her baby on a cradleboard strapped to her back, while the man poses on horseback.

PEOPLE OF THE NORTHERN GREAT PLAINS

IN ADDITION TO THE OGLALAS AND THE MINICONJOUS, THERE WERE FIVE OTHER BANDS THAT MADE UP THE LAKOTA PEOPLE: THE HUNKPAPAS, THE TWO KETTLES, THE BLACKFEET, THE BRULÉ, AND THE SANS ARCS. THE LAKOTAS, PART OF A LARGER GROUP CALLED THE GREAT SIOUX NATION AND SOMETIMES SIMPLY CALLED THE SIOUX, WERE THE MOST POWERFUL PEOPLE ON THE NORTHERN PLAINS WHEN CRAZY HORSE WAS A BOY. THEIR TERRITORY RANGED FROM WHAT IS NOW SOUTH DAKOTA INTO PARTS OF NEBRASKA, WYOMING, AND NORTH DAKOTA. NEIGHBORING PEOPLE INCLUDED THEIR **ALLIES**, THE CHEYENNES AND ARAPAHOS, AS WELL AS RIVALS, THE PAWNEE AND CROWS.

THE VISION

When Crazy Horse was around 14, he went on a vision quest. With the help of a holy man, Crazy Horse took part in an *Inipi*, which is a Lakota **purification** ceremony that takes place in a sweat lodge built from willow saplings and covered in animal skins. Crazy Horse then rode into the wilderness, where he stayed alone for four days. There, he **fasted** and prayed.

According to legend, Crazy Horse had a vision in which he saw a man riding a horse during a storm. The man had a lightning bolt painted on his cheek and a small stone in his ear. Crazy Horse shared his vision with the Lakota holy man as well as his father, who felt the dream meant his son was **destined** to become a great warrior.

Traditional *Inipi* were made from branches and animal skins. Today, modern sweat lodges such as the one pictured here can be draped with blankets or other materials.

SEEKING VISIONS

IN TRADITIONAL LAKOTA CULTURE, IT WAS COMMON FOR YOUNG BOYS TO UNDERTAKE VISION QUESTS. A VISION QUEST IS A PERIOD OF TIME IN WHICH A PERSON SEEKS TO RECEIVE A VISION, WHICH IS A SPIRITUAL EXPERIENCE. DURING A VISION QUEST, THE SEEKER IS ALONE AND FAST FOR BETWEEN ONE AND FOUR DAYS. HE MAY SEE A SPIRITUAL BEING OR ANIMAL THAT IS IMPORTANT TO HIS LIFE OR MAY RECEIVE GUIDANCE REGARDING WHICH PATH HIS LIFE WILL TAKE. VISION QUESTS WERE CONSIDERED A **RITE** OF PASSAGE FOR THE LAKOTA PEOPLE.

GOING ON THE WARPATH

Crazy Horse joined his first war party in 1857 during an attack against a Pawnee village in eastern Nebraska. Riding into battle far ahead of the others, the young warrior showed incredible bravery and skill. According to his cousin, a man named Eagle Elk, Crazy Horse's efforts during this battle caused people to take note of him. He proved himself again in fights against the Atsinas and Crows.

As Crazy Horse's **reputation** grew, he developed a band of loyal followers who joined his war parties. People were drawn to him, although many found him to be a **solitary** and quiet man who often preferred to wander off on his own. As a leader, he became known for careful battle **strategies**.

Animals were very important to the Lakota people. Crazy Horse prized hawks, such as the red-tailed hawk shown here.

GUARDIAN SPIRIT

THE RED-TAILED HAWK WAS IMPORTANT TO CRAZY HORSE'S LIFE. HE SAW THE MAGNIFICENT BIRD IN HIS FIRST VISION QUEST, AND FROM THEN ON REGARDED IT AS HIS "GUARDIAN SPIRIT." CRAZY HORSE VALUED THE HAWK FOR ITS FOCUSED HUNTING BEHAVIOR AND FOR ITS SWIFTNESS AND POWER. CRAZY HORSE OFTEN WORE TWO OR THREE HAWK FEATHERS ON HIS HEAD, AND WAS ONCE REPORTED TO HAVE TIED A HAWK'S BODY TO HIS HAIR DURING AN IMPORTANT BATTLE.

FIGHTING FOR LAKOTA LAND

Beginning in the mid-1800s, white settlers began traveling west in large numbers. Many passed through or settled on Lakota territory. From the time he was young, Crazy Horse learned to distrust their presence and the U.S. government that supported it.

In the 1860s, Crazy Horse joined forces with the Oglala warrior Red Cloud, who declared war against white settlement along the Bozeman Trail. Crazy Horse led **raids** against settlers and soldiers, attacking trading posts, ranches, wagon trains, and forts.

THE BOZEMAN TRAIL

THE LAKOTAS AND OTHER GREAT PLAINS PEOPLE HAD LEARNED NOT TO TRUST WHITE SETTLERS AFTER THOUSANDS OF NATIVE PEOPLE DIED OF SMALLPOX, A PREVIOUSLY UNKNOWN ILLNESS, IN THE 1830S. IN 1863, TWO WHITE **PROSPECTORS** OPENED A NEW PATH FROM THE OREGON TRAIL INTO THE GOLDFIELDS OF MONTANA. CALLED THE BOZEMAN TRAIL, THE PATH CUT THROUGH THE LAKOTAS' MOST VALUABLE HUNTING GROUNDS, RUINING THE GRASS THAT FED THEIR ANIMALS, SCARING AWAY BISON, AND CHANGING THEIR WAYS OF LIFE.

In December 1866, Crazy Horse helped attack Fort Phil Kearny in Wyoming. Heading a group of **decoy** warriors, he skillfully drew a troop of U.S. soldiers from the safety of their fort. Lakota, Arapaho, and Cheyenne warriors ambushed the unsuspecting soldiers, killing 81 men.

FORT PHIL KEARNY

FORT PHILIP KEARNEY

The soldiers at Fort Phil Kearny were led by William J. Fetterman. The events that occurred at the fort in 1866 later became known as the Fetterman **Massacre**.

RESISTING THE RESERVATION

In 1868, the U.S. government and the Sioux people signed the Fort Laramie Treaty at Fort Laramie in Wyoming. According to the treaty, the U.S. government would close the Bozeman Trail and its forts along that road in exchange for peace.

The treaty created the Great Sioux **Reservation**, which included the Black Hills. The government promised these sacred lands would belong to the Sioux people forever. Red Cloud was promised his own reservation, which was also called an agency, where the government would supply his people with seeds, cattle, tools, and training to become farmers.

Crazy Horse resisted the move. Living on a reservation would mean giving up the traditional Lakota ways of life and would make him and his people dependent on the U.S. government.

General William Tecumseh Sherman meets with tribal representatives at Fort Laramie in 1868 to work on the treaty that would end Red Cloud's War. The site of several important Indian treaties, Fort Laramie is now a National Historic Site.

SHIRT WEARER

AROUND THE TIME OF RED CLOUD'S WAR, CRAZY HORSE WAS SELECTED AS ONE OF FOUR SHIRT WEARERS, OR HEAD WARRIORS, OF THE OGLALAS. THIS WAS ONE OF THE HIGHEST HONORS AN OGLALA COULD EARN. THE HONOR WAS GIVEN TO TWO TO FOUR MEN, WHO WERE SEEN AS EQUALS, WHOSE BRAVERY HELPED WIN IMPORTANT WARS FOR THEIR PEOPLE. IN BECOMING A SHIRT WEARER, CRAZY HORSE BECAME RESPONSIBLE FOR SELECTING CAMPSITES AND HUNTING GROUNDS, SETTLING DISAGREEMENTS, MAKING IMPORTANT DECISIONS, AND TAKING CARE OF THE POOR IN HIS COMMUNITY.

THE BATTLE FOR THE BLACK HILLS

Despite a promise of peace, trouble came for Crazy Horse and the Lakotas again. An expedition led by Lieutenant Colonel George Armstrong Custer discovered gold in the Black Hills in 1874. Despite the promises set forth in the Fort Laramie Treaty, more prospectors settled on the Lakotas' sacred land. The U.S. Army was sent to the area, too.

In 1875, the U.S. government made an offer to buy the Black Hills. When the Lakotas refused, the government cast aside the Fort Laramie Treaty and said any Lakota who did not move to a reservation would be considered **hostile**. Crazy Horse, alongside the great chiefs Sitting Bull and Gall, led a band of Lakotas and Cheyennes who refused to leave their homeland. In early 1876, the U.S. Army began a series of attacks to force them onto reservations.

SITTING BULL

SITTING BULL WAS PERHAPS 10 YEARS OLDER THAN CRAZY HORSE. HE WAS BORN AROUND 1831 IN WHAT IS NOW SOUTH DAKOTA. A MEMBER OF THE HUNKPAPA BAND OF LAKOTAS, HE WAS A SKILLFUL HUNTER AND WARRIOR EARLY IN LIFE. LIKE CRAZY HORSE, HE WAS KNOWN FOR HIS WISH TO AVOID CONTACT WITH WHITES AND TO LIVE IN THE TRADITIONAL WAY. SITTING BULL WAS SAID TO BE GUIDED BY POWERFUL VISIONS, WHICH GAVE HIM EXTRAORDINARY COURAGE ON THE BATTLEFIELD.

Chief Sitting Bull, shown here in 1881, was a great leader of the Lakota and Cheyenne people that refused to give up their land to the United States.

VICTORY AT THE ROSEBUD AND THE LITTLE BIGHORN

On June 17, 1876, **Brigadier** General George Crook led more than 1,000 soldiers to advance along Rosebud Creek in present-day Montana. They were trying to reach Sitting Bull's encampment at the Little Bighorn River.

Crazy Horse met the troops with around 1,500 warriors under his charge. He attacked the enemy's weak points, scattering the soldiers and forcing Crook and his troops to retreat to Wyoming.

Crazy Horse's victory at the Battle of the Rosebud hurt the army's forces, but the United States continued fighting. More than a week later, on June 25, Lieutenant Colonel Custer led the U.S. Seventh **Cavalry** during what's now called the Battle of the Little Bighorn.

GENERAL GEORGE CROOK

A drawing from around 1900 by Lakota artist Amos Bad Heart Buffalo depicts warriors at the Battle of the Little Bighorn.

Custer led his soldiers against Lakotas and Cheyennes who were camped along the Little Bighorn River. There were 5,000 to 8,000 people camped there, and around 1,500 were warriors. Although those in the camp were surprised by the attack, they outnumbered U.S. forces and fought back skillfully. Under the command of Crazy Horse and Gall, warriors on horseback surrounded Custer's troops and killed almost a third of them.

The Battle of the Little Bighorn became known as "Custer's Last Stand." It's one of the most famous fights of the western frontier. Furious at the defeat, the U.S. military took control of all the Lakota reservations, treating those living there as prisoners of war. The government also passed a law that took the Black Hills and the Powder River country away from the Great Sioux Reservation.

LIEUTENANT COLONEL CUSTER

CONTINUING THE FIGHT

AFTER THE INDIAN VICTORY AT THE LITTLE BIGHORN, THE ARMY STEPPED UP ITS EFFORTS AGAINST CRAZY HORSE AND HIS ALLIES. IN THE FACE OF CONTINUED ARMY ATTACKS, SITTING BULL AND GALL ESCAPED TO CANADA WITH THOUSANDS OF FOLLOWERS. CRAZY HORSE REFUSED TO LEAVE HIS HOMELAND, HOWEVER, AND MANY LAKOTAS CHOSE TO CONTINUE THE FIGHT AT HIS SIDE. THROUGHOUT THE SUMMER AND INTO THE NEXT WINTER, HE LED A BAND OF LAKOTAS AND THEIR ALLIES AGAINST CONSTANT ATTACKS BY U.S. FORCES.

BATTLE OF THE LITTLE BIGHORN

Lieutenant Colonel Custer was known among native groups of the Great Plains after he led a massacre at a peaceful Cheyenne village on the Washita River in 1868. Under his command, the army killed more than 100 men, women, and children.

THE REBEL SURRENDERS

From 1876 to 1877, Crazy Horse and his people suffered continued harassment by the U.S. Army, along with a harsh winter. Crazy Horse realized he could no longer keep his followers safe on the run. In May 1877, he brought his group to the Red Cloud Agency at Fort Robinson, Nebraska, and surrendered.

Army officials and agency leaders still didn't trust Crazy Horse. It was reported in August 1877 that Crazy Horse vowed to continue to fight American forces, but his words may have been translated incorrectly. Similarly, someone told General George Crook that Crazy Horse promised to kill him when Crook came to Fort Robinson on military orders.

In a copy of an engraving from 1877, the Sioux people travel to surrender to U.S. forces at Red Cloud Agency in Nebraska.

THE KILLING OF CRAZY HORSE

Despite surrendering to U.S. forces, Crazy Horse tried to keep his independence. After a few months of living on the reservation, Crazy Horse left without permission to take his sick wife to another reservation that was about 40 miles (64 km) away. General Crook took it as a sign that Crazy Horse was escaping to return to battle and ordered his arrest.

Crazy Horse was arrested on September 5, and he didn't resist at first. An army captain and reservation police led him to the prison at Fort Robinson. There are many versions of what happened next, and what actually happened is unclear. One report says that once Crazy Horse saw the inside of the prison, he began resisting. Someone stabbed him in the stomach, and he died that same night.

Today, a monument marks the spot where Crazy Horse was killed in 1877.

AFTER THE DEATH OF CRAZY HORSE

THE FIGHT THAT CRAZY HORSE AND SITTING BULL LED PROVED TO BE THE LAST GREAT STAND OF THE FREE LAKOTAS. IN FALL 1877, THE U.S. GOVERNMENT TOOK THE REST OF LAKOTA LAND IN NEBRASKA, FORCING THEM TO MOVE TO A NEW RESERVATION ON LAND ALONG THE MISSOURI RIVER. SITTING BULL RETURNED FROM CANADA IN 1881 AND LIVED ON THE RESERVATION, WHERE HE CONTINUED TO SPEAK OUT AGAINST THE GOVERNMENT'S UNFAIR PRACTICES. HE WAS KILLED IN 1890 AS RESERVATION POLICE TRIED TO ARREST HIM.

ON THIS SPOT
CRAZY HORSE
OGALLALA CHIEF
WAS KILLED
SEPT. 5 1877

CARVING A MOUNTAIN

In 1939, the Oglala chief Henry Standing Bear commissioned a memorial to Crazy Horse in the Black Hills that would rival the giant carving of U.S. presidents on nearby Mount Rushmore. He invited Korczak Ziolkowski, a Polish American sculptor who had worked on Mount Rushmore, to create this tribute to all North American Indians. After nearly a decade of planning, Ziolkowski made his first blast into the mountain in 1948. Five survivors of the Battle of the Little Bighorn attended the opening ceremony.

When the Crazy Horse Memorial is complete, it will be the largest mountain carving in the world, standing 641 feet (195 m) across and 563 feet (172 m) high. Although Ziolkowski died in 1982 and his wife in 2014, his children and grandchildren continue to work on the project. As of 2015, only Crazy Horse's face is complete.

IN MANY WAYS, THE HUGE SCULPTURE OF CRAZY HORSE IS A STRANGE WAY TO PAY TRIBUTE TO SUCH A MODEST MAN, WHO REVERED THE LAND AND AVOIDED WHITE MEN AND THEIR CAMERAS THROUGHOUT HIS LIFE. NO PHOTOGRAPHS OF HIM EXIST TODAY, YET DESCRIPTIONS FROM THOSE WHO KNEW THE LEGENDARY WARRIOR HAVE SURVIVED. HE WAS SAID TO BE ABOUT 5 FEET 8 INCHES (1.7 M) TALL, WITH WAIST-LENGTH, WAVY BROWN HAIR.

The great size of the Crazy Horse Memorial makes it easy to spot from a distance.

A LEGACY OF RESISTANCE

In the many years that have passed since Crazy Horse lived, his name still stands among his people as a symbol of resistance and a willingness to fight for freedom and the traditional Lakota ways.

In the 1970s, the American Indian Movement took inspiration from Crazy Horse as it fought the U.S. government's attempts to mine uranium on what was left of Lakota land. A group of Lakotas also brought a lawsuit against the United States to have the Black Hills returned to their people. In 1980, the Supreme Court awarded the Sioux Nation more than $100 million in compensation for the loss of the Black Hills. That award is now worth around $1.3 billion, but the Sioux refuse to take the money. Many believe in what Crazy Horse fought for: that the Black Hills are not for sale.

BLACK HILLS, SOUTH DAKOTA

A TIMELINE OF CRAZY HORSE'S LIFE

ca. 1840 Crazy Horse, known then as Curly Hair, is born in present-day South Dakota.

ca. 1854 Crazy Horse experiences his first vision quest.

1863 The Bozeman Trail opens to settlers and prospectors, though Native American groups in the area had used the land for thousands of years prior.

ca. 1864 Crazy Horse joins Red Cloud in his war to protest settlement along the Bozeman Trail.

1868 The Sioux and the U.S. government sign the Fort Laramie Treaty, bringing an end to Red Cloud's War, closing forts along the Bozeman Trail, and promising the Black Hills to the Sioux forever.

1874 Prospectors discover gold in the Black Hills.

1875 The U.S. government offers to buy the Black Hills. The Lakotas refuse, prompting the government to order them onto reservations.

JUNE 17, 1876 Crazy Horse defeats U.S. forces at the Battle of the Rosebud.

JULY 25, 1876 Lakota and Cheyenne forces defeat George Armstrong Custer's forces during the Battle of the Little Bighorn.

1877 Congress repeals the Fort Laramie Treaty and takes the Black Hills from the Sioux. The Lakotas and other native groups are forced onto reservations.

MAY 1877 Crazy Horse surrenders at Fort Robinson, Nebraska.

SEPTEMBER 5, 1877 Crazy Horse dies from stab wounds.

1939 Henry Standing Bear commissions the Crazy Horse Memorial.

GLOSSARY

ally: A person or group of people that agrees to help another group of people.

brigadier: A rank in the army.

cavalry: In the past, soldiers who fought on horseback.

decoy: An object used to draw attention away from something.

destined: Developing as though according to plan.

fast: To give up food and water for a certain period of time.

hostile: Unfriendly.

massacre: A brutal killing of a large number of people.

prospector: A person who searches for gold or other minerals.

purification: The act of making something very pure or clean.

raid: A sudden attack on an enemy.

reputation: A widely held belief about someone or something.

reservation: Land set aside by the government for a specific Native American group or groups to live on.

rite: An act done for a special purpose, often having to do with religion.

solitary: Done or existing alone.

strategy: A plan of action.

traditional: Passed down over many years.

INDEX

WEBSITES

Due to the changing nature of Internet links, PowerKids Press has developed an online list of websites related to the subject of this book. This site is updated regularly. Please use this link to access the list: www.powerkidslinks.com/natv/crzy